Feng Shui: A Practical Guide
by Richard Taylor and Wang Tann

Have you ever considered that the mirror on your bedroom wall is bringing you bad luck or worse, bad health? That the way you arrange your furniture can welcome prosperity into your life? That the direction your home or apartment is facing may indicate your fate?

Feng Shui is an ancient Chinese method for creating balance between our lives and our surroundings. This practical guide will teach you how to live harmoniously within your own environment.

Step-by-step, utilizing examples and illustrations, this informative guide shows you everything you need to know about lines of energy - the good and the bad. It will even instruct you on how to design and build a home, office, or other interior space.

Richard Taylor is an economist, consulting with corporations in Asia. Hong Kong-born Wang Tann is a Feng Shui master, as were his father, grandfather, and ancestors.

ASTROLOG - THE HEALING SERIES

Holistic Healing
Rachel Lewin

Feng Shui
Richard Taylor and Wang Tann

Reiki
Bill Waites and Master Naharo

Bach Flower Remedies
David Lord

Aromatherapy
Marion Wayman

Reflexology
Nathan B. Strauss

Shiatsu
Nathan B. Strauss

Feng Shui

A Practical Guide

Richard Taylor & Wang Tann

Astrolog Publishing House

P.O. Box 1123, Hod Hasharon 45111, Israel

TEL. 972-9-7412044

FAX. 972-9-7442714

E-Mail: info@astrolog.co.il

Astrolog Web Site: www.astrolog.co.il

ISBN 965-494-044-2

Published by Astrolog Publishing House 1998

Printed in Israel

10 9 8 7 6 5 4 3 2 1

風
水

Introduction

About seven years ago, I went to Hong Kong in order to examine the financial situation of a company that supplied irrigation and fertilizer equipment to China. Unlike its other Asian branches, which were making enormous profits, the Hong Kong branch, which was responsible for the whole of China, was losing money. I spent two weeks in an elegant office, scrutinizing papers and reports, examining a few price estimates, and trying to figure out why everyone else in our field was succeeding, whereas we were having such a hard time. I was particularly puzzled by the success of foreign companies who were purchasing their equipment and knowledge from us and charging higher prices than we were.

As I failed to find the key to this mystery among the papers, I finally approached the people involved.

One afternoon, I took the chief clerk, a Chinese man in his forties called Wang Tann, out to lunch. Over bowls of steaming Chinese delicacies, I asked him why the business was not functioning properly. I pointed out to him that despite the superb quality of our products, our low prices, and the location of our offices and showrooms in an elegant building right in the center of Hong Kong, we were still, incredibly, suffering from a serious lack of clients and potential clients.

Wang Tann hesitated, squirmed uneasily in his seat, and answered evasively. Clearly, something was bothering him. The Chinese are by nature loyal to their employers, and here I was, a foreigner, finding fault with his direct superior. Finally, when I made it clear that unless the situation changed, we would be obliged to shut down the office, it all came out.

"It's all because of the office," Wang Tann mumbled. "Nothing is planned according to the rules of Feng Shui."

"Feng Shui?" Although I was not unfamiliar with Chinese culture, the term was new to me.

"It is of the utmost importance in business, particularly when our clients are Chinese peasants. Feng Shui teaches us exactly how to design our houses, offices and family burial plots, and where to locate them, so that we may be blessed with good fortune."

At this point, the Chinese clerk began to get excited, and he spread out a paper napkin and drew various signs on it. I lost my train of thought.

To make a long story short, that was my first encounter with the term *Feng Shui*. Wang Tann brought his uncle, a "Feng Shui Master," who redesigned the office, arranged for a fountain to be placed in front of the main entrance to the building, relocated the rest-rooms at the back of the office, hung a few bells and screens, and installed some lamps which gave out a particularly bright light in the main showroom. Three months later, I departed from Hong Kong, leaving behind me an office which was well on the way to success.

This book is based on the main principles of Feng Shui, as they were dictated by the Master to his nephew Wang Tann, and written down by the latter in some twenty notebooks. It is also based on a dozen or so audio tapes in which the Master himself lectured in poor English, as well as on everything I have gleaned from scores of books on the subject.

The purpose of this book is to teach Westerners the principles of the ancient teachings of Feng Shui, so that they will be able to use it to their own advantage in a simple, logical way.

May the dragon, the tiger, the phoenix and the tortoise follow the instructions of the snake and may you be protected from evil. (If you do not understand the meaning of this blessing, then you must read this book.)

What is Feng Shui?

Literally, *Feng Shui* means "wind and water." It consists of the two fundamental elements of nature, or the universe, which involve movement of energy. Through the flow of energy, these two elements are capable of shaping the ground, the earth, human environment and, above all, the currents of energy that dominate man's surroundings (that is, the *chi*, as we shall see later on).

Wind, when it means air, is the most important element in human life. Even a strong, fit person cannot survive more than a few minutes without air. Water is the next in line: without it one can only survive for a few days at most.

When broken down to its two components, Feng Shui means "wind and water." Yet the term as a whole expresses much more: It refers to the flow of energy throughout the entire universe.

The choice of a term which consists of the combination of two elements is also important. Chinese philosophy as a whole is based on the principle of harmony or equilibrium which is achieved through a balance of various components (like the balance between *yin* and *yang*, which will be discussed later). Still, this is not about the harmony between wind and water, but rather about the harmony between the energetic forces of nature, and between these forces and the environment in which they operate.

Let us forget for a moment about Feng Shui, which affects man's physical environment, and turn to the human body itself. Chinese medicine regards the meridians, or channels through which the life energy, or *chi*, flows, as the most important system in the human body. There are many sub-systems of meridians in the body, and each meridian has many key points. A person will remain vital and healthy as long as the chi flows unimpaired through its proper channel. Once a chi channel is blocked, the flow of energy is impaired, and the blockage must be removed by means of the use of needles, massage or herbs, in order for the person to be cured.

It is important to note that the complex meridian system which carries the chi is invisible. Unlike blood vessels or bones, it cannot be seen. Yet we are aware of its existence, employ various means and powers to keep it functioning properly, and learn how to use it from books and in special schools.

Although there is no "scientific" way to see or measure

the flow of chi energy through the body, there is hardly a person in the West today who is not aware of meridians, chi or the healing methods of Chinese medicine.

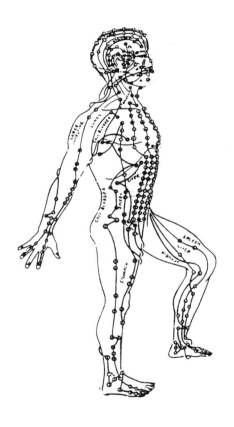

This is also true of the environment, or the earth itself. Above and below ground, there is a complex system of "channels" which carry the chi. The system of chi channels affects and is affected by the terrain, and exists everywhere: on mountain-tops and in the desert, at home and in the office, along rivers and deep inside caves.

Moreover, just like the system of meridians and chi within the body, the chi channels of the natural environment also follow a set of rules which are crucial in case of blockages and breakdowns. The Feng Shui system, too, follows a set of rules of its own.

Feng Shui deals with the energy system of the natural environment.

Feng Shui teaches us how to live in harmony with environmental energy.

Feng Shui teaches us how to create a balance between the various energies of nature, which together form environmental energy.

Feng Shui teaches us to locate and map the energy flow lines in the environment.

Feng Shui shows us how to differentiate positive energy from negative energy.

Feng Shui shows us how to position the house, the grave, the office, and so on, so that they are in harmony with the flow of energy in nature.

Feng Shui shows us where to position ourselves in order to absorb the flow of positive energy and avoid the negative flow.

Feng Shui prevents us from staying in places where negative energy flows, yet shows us the way to correct this flow and the quite simple means by which negative energy can be turned into positive energy.

To conclude this part of our discussion, let us stress something that will be elaborated upon later: Feng Shui encompasses not only the environment, but also the people who live in it. We shall later relate to the significance of the Chinese calendar and a person's date of birth within the overall system of Feng Shui. Thus, Feng Shui combines internal energy which flows in the meridians with the general flow of energy in the natural environment. In other words, man is a microcosm which is both affected by its surroundings and at the same time affects the environment and the flow of chi in it.

What is Feng Shui based on?

Feng Shui is in fact the final product, philosophically and practically speaking, of a Chinese doctrine that goes back 7,000 years. (It probably originated even before that.)

The Chinese define Feng Shui as "the art of finding the proper place." The Masters employ various ground patterns and signs which derive from Chinese philosophy and the Chinese concept of life and the universe. In order to understand these principles, we shall discuss such inter-related terms as *chi*, *yin* and *yang*, *t'ai chi* and the five elements.

"This (good conduct) is the foundation of long life. Just as the breath of the blue sky (is calm), so the will and the heart of those who are pure will be in peace, and the breath of Yang will be stable in those who keep themselves in harmony with nature. Even if there are noxious spirits they cannot cause injury to those who follow the laws of the seasons. Therefore the sages preserved the natural spirit and were in harmony with the breath of Heaven, and were thus in direct communication with Heaven."

(*The Yellow Emperor's Classic of Internal Medicine*, translated by Ilza Veith, University of California Press)

Chi

Chi is the beginning of all things. Chinese philosophy says nothing more about it. In his book "Tao I Ching," which lays the foundations for Taoism, Lao Tse relates to chi as follows: "He who speaks of it knows it not, and he who knows it speaks not." In other words, as it is not to be seen nor spoken of, the existence of chi cannot be proved. If you do not believe in the existence of chi, there is no point going on reading this book.

Chi is not something that can be analyzed by human faculties. Chi exists beyond existence and non-existence; it is eternal and unchanging, yet changes constantly; it is all and it is nothing; it contains all and is contained by all.

Still, how can we humans know that chi exists?

We learn of chi from the great principle which governs the universe, according to which all things are born, develop, mature, die and disappear.

Chi is expressed graphically in the form of an empty circle. To make it easier to understand, we shall refer to chi as energy.

> "From eternal non-existence, therefore, we serenely observe the mysterious beginning of the Universe;
> From eternal existence we clearly see the apparent distinctions."
> (Tao Te Ching, translated by Ch'u Ta-Kao)

T'ai Chi

Closely related to chi is *t'ai chi*, which is in fact the name of the well-known yin/yang symbol. According to the principles of Feng Shui, t'ai chi is "the pool where all things merge," that is, where yin and yang affect the actual flowing of the chi energy by their differences and similarities.

Tao

The *tao* principle is in fact similar to the idea mentioned in the above paragraph, whereby everything travels along a path which begins at birth and ends with death. There is a tao for the world, which means the way of the world, and there is a human tao: a tao for warriors, a tao for women, a tao for carpenters, etc. Once a person's tao is in harmony with the tao of the world, he lives happily and peacefully, fulfilling himself completely. When clashes occur between the universal tao and the personal tao, then the person involved is bound to stray from his designated path.

Tao is just like a seed within the chi. The Chinese express the chi graphically as a womb, while tao, which is in fact the concept behind the journey, is depicted in the form of a dot in the centre of the chi.

"Infinite profundity is the gate whence comes the beginning of all parts of the Universe."

(Tao Te Ching, translated by Ch'u Ta-Kao)

Yin/Yang

Although it opposes Western philosophy, the concept of *yin/yang* is well known today in the West. The Chinese believe that everything in the world tends toward either yin or yang, darkness or light, feminine or masculine, negative or positive.

It is important to note the word "tends." Nothing in the world is completely yin or completely yang. Even the most prominently masculine yang expressions tend to have a feminine yin element about them. In everything there is both yin and yang, which should be balanced. (Feng Shui, in fact, attempts to achieve that state of balance.) When something is more yin, it is defined as yin. When it is more yang, it is defined as yang. Although the two components, or principles, are total opposites, they nevertheless complement each other.

We mentioned earlier that yin is the negative feminine element, whereas yang is the positive masculine element. It is important to note that the terms "positive" and "negative" are by no means parallel to "good" and "bad." Rather, they stand for opposite poles, not unlike the poles of a magnet. Together, the positive pole and the negative pole create the whole magnetic field.

The following traits are associated with yin: feminine, negative, passive, submissive, follower, dark, earthly, emotional, square, low, earth, moon, night, stagnant, beneath, soft, cold, water, mother, daughter, back, sour, sad, etc.

The following traits are associated with yang: masculine, positive, active, firm, leader, bright, spiritual, rational, round, tall, sky, sun, day, movement, above, hard, hot, fire, father, son, front, sweet, angry, etc.

It is important to remember that both yin and yang originate from the same seed of chi, as can be seen in the Chinese spelling of the two words. The first letter (on the left) is identical in both cases and means "hill."

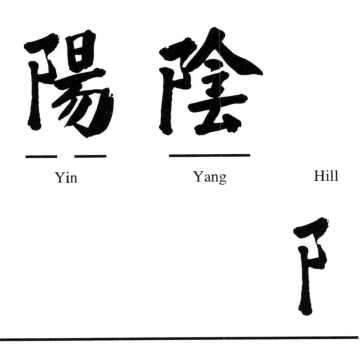

Yin   Yang   Hill

To recap: The essence of Feng Shui, put simply, is the balance of the flow of yin and yang in man's natural environment, as well as between man and his natural environment. This harmony is the essence of everything.

The common Chinese sign for yin is a broken line:

━━ ━━ .

The common Chinese sign for yang is a solid line:

━━━━━ .

When these lines are placed on top of one another, they first create the trigrams and then the hexagrams which we know from the *I Ching*.

Trigrams and the Pah Kwa charm*

As mentioned above, we have two signs: a solid line representing the yang, and a broken line representing the yin. If the lines are used to form pairs, the following four combinations are produced:

Two yin lines one on top of the other represent winter.

A yang line above a yin line represents fall.

A yin line above a yang line represents spring.

Two yang lines on top of one another represent summer.

*There are different transliterations of the Chinese names and concepts. We can find, for example, *pah kwa* written as *pa kua*, *pa che*, etc. The same is true for other concepts.

Let us now add yet another line to form a trigram, so that a system of eight different combinations is produced:

This trigram, composed of three yin lines, represents the Earth.

This trigram, composed of one yang line above two yin lines, represents the Mountain.

This trigram, composed of one yang line between two yin lines, represents Water.

This trigram, composed of one yin line beneath two yang lines, represents the Wind.

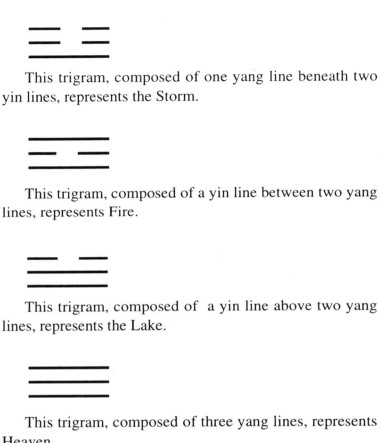

This trigram, composed of one yang line beneath two yin lines, represents the Storm.

This trigram, composed of a yin line between two yang lines, represents Fire.

This trigram, composed of a yin line above two yang lines, represents the Lake.

This trigram, composed of three yang lines, represents Heaven.

Clearly, at both ends we have absolute yin (Earth) and absolute yang (Heaven), whereas the sequence between them is marked by varying ratios (locations) and amounts of yin/yang.

The development from the original chi to the trigrams, which are in fact the actual expression of Feng Shui , may be described graphically:

Tao

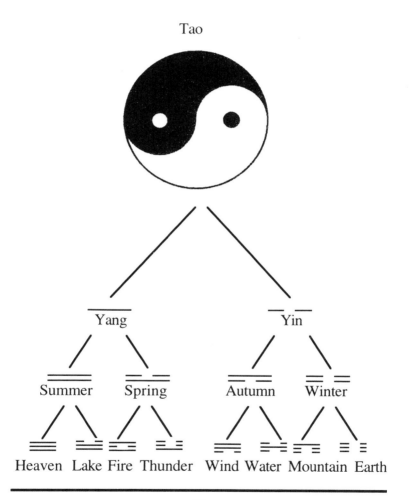

The eight trigrams are of great importance to Feng Shui, as each represents an essence, a direction, a family member, an hour of the day, etc. Let us go over the names and traits associated with the eight trigrams and then sum it all up in a single table which should be memorized.

Earth

This trigram, composed of three broken, negative yin lines, represents the force which stands in opposition to Heaven. It is therefore called "Earth" and is defined as "passive." The earth is dark and has no life of its own, yet it sustains all forms of life which, when fertilized by the heavenly light, come out into the open to create the world. Within the family of trigrams, this one stands for the Mother, who gives birth, nourishes and devotes herself to her children. Within the animal world, it stands for the mare (and sometimes for the cow); within the human body, it represents the stomach; on the calendar, it corresponds to the beginning of fall and, among the eight directions, stands for south-west. The color associated with this trigram is black, and it is associated with the element of Earth.

Mountain

Having climbed up, the yang line reaches the top of the trigram and is unable to go further. At the same time, this trigram represents a solid masculine element resting heavily on two feminine lines, not unlike a mountain which rests upon the earth. This trigram is therefore called "Mountain" and is associated with "stillness" (or "lack of movement"). The mountain stands in the way of travelers, yet contains many treasures which only the wise can reveal. At the top of the mountain, one can be alone, far from the madding crowd, and fill one's lungs with clean air. This trigram, therefore, sometimes stands for raw potential not fully realized, or for a blockage, barrier, or dead end. Within the family of trigrams, it represents the youngest son; within the animal world - the dog, and within the human body - the hand (or finger). The color associated with this trigram is green; it is associated with the element of earth, its direction is north-east, and its season is late winter/early spring.

Water

This trigram, composed of a yang line between two yin lines, is called "Water," described as "abyss" and means "danger." Water flows over the earth, powerfully sweeping everything that stands in its way. He who knows how to control the flow of water and direct it according to his own will can benefit from its immense power, but those who stand weak and unprepared in its way will meet with disaster. Within the family of trigrams, this is considered as the middle son; within the human body, it represents the ear, and within the animal world - the pig; its direction is north, its color is red, and the season associated with it is winter, when heavy rains fall and cover the earth with water.

Wind

This trigram, consisting of a feminine yin line gently penetrating the masculine yang state, is called "Wind," and represents the ability of delicate elements to penetrate solid obstacles, just like the wind carries pollen, spreading it over the earth, or the tree slowly sends its roots into the rocks. Within the family of trigrams, it represents the eldest daughter; within the human body, it stands for the thigh (and sometimes for the arm as well), and within the animal world, it represents the rooster. The color of the trigram is white, the element associated with it is wood, its direction is south-east, and the season characterizing it is early summer.

Storm
(Thunder)

This trigram is marked by the emergence of a yang line upward into an existing state, thereby creating a movement which is referred to as "Storm" and described as "awakening." (Trigrams start at the bottom, so that the appearance of a masculine line below two feminine lines - or vice versa - is defined as "emergence.") The storm causes an upheaval in the world and catalyzes processes, so that when it dies down, nothing is as it used to be. Within the family of trigrams, it represents the eldest son; within the animal world, it represents the dragon (and sometimes the galloping horse), and within the human body, it stands for the legs. The direction of this trigram is east and the season associated with it is spring, when the world is awakened from the long winter sleep by the heavenly force which penetrates the earth. The color of this trigram is orange, and it is associated with the element of wood.

Fire

Composed of a single feminine yin line between two yang lines, this trigram is called "Fire" and is associated with the word "clinging" and with the following traits: brilliance, beauty, warmth, restlessness and mental clarity. It represents the middle daughter, the pheasant and the human eye. Its direction is south, its color is yellow and the season associated with it is summer, when the sun is a ball of fire at its zenith and everything in nature is gloriously in full bloom.

Lake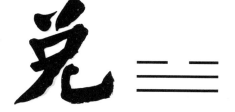

The youngest daughter in the family of trigrams is represented by a single yin line resting on two yang lines. The name of this trigram is "Lake," and the traits associated with it are "joy" (radiating from the sparkling water of the lake) and "tranquillity" (typical of deep, still water). Sometimes the water becomes stagnant and gives off an odor which endows this trigram with yet another name: "Bog." The season associated with this trigram is early fall, when the joy of the harvest is mixed with the sadness engendered by the approach of winter. The color of this trigram is blue, its direction is west, and it represents the sheep and the human mouth.

Heaven

This trigram, composed of three solid, positive yang lines, is called "Heaven" and described as "Creator." It represents the pure positive power of the sky which, by giving light to the world, fertilizes it and creates the spark of life. This trigram, representing the father of the family, also stands for the horse and for the human head. The season associated with it is late summer and its direction is north-west. The color of the trigram is purple, and the element associated with it is metal.

The following table sums up the meanings associated with the trigrams and is of great importance to the practice of Feng Shui:

Trigram	☴	☳	☲
Chinese Name	Sun	Chen	Li
Name	Wind	Storm	Fire
Adjective	The Gentle	The Arousing	The Clinging
Relationship	Yin/Yang/Yang	Yang/Yin/Yin	Yang/Yin/Yang
Element	Wood	Wood	Fire
Status	Eldest Daughter	Eldest Son	Middle Daughter
Direction	South-East	East	South
Number	4	3	9
Life Area	Penetration	Arousal	Lightness
Area in Family Life	Wealth	Health	Consciousness,
Behavioral Characteristic	Simplification	Upheaval	Honor Warmth
Seasons	Beginning of Summer	Spring	Summer
Time of Day	Beginning of Day	Morning	Noon
Animal World	Cock	Dragon	Pheasant
Man's Body	Thigh	Legs	Eye
Color	White	Orange	Yellow
Symbol	Wind	Thunder (Storm)	Fire
Character	Gentleness	Arousal	Clinging

Trigram	☷	☶	☵
Chinese Name	K'un	Ken	K'an
Name	Earth	Mountain	Water
Adjective	The Receptive	Keeping Still	The Abysmal
Relationship	All Yin	Yin/Yin/Yang	Yin/Yang/Yin
Element	Earth	Earth	Water
Status	Mother	Youngest Son	Middle Son
Direction	South-West	North-East	North
Number	2	8	1
Life Area	Fertility	Potential	Movement
Area in Family Life	Prosperity	Education	Career
Behavioral Characteristic	Creation	Obstacle	Change
Seasons	Beginning of Fall	End of Winter, Beginning of Spring	Winter
Time of Day	Afternoon	Dawn	Night
Animal World	Mare	Dog	Pig
Man's Body	Abdomen	Palm of Hand	Ear
Color	Black	Green	Red
Symbol	Earth	Mountain	Water
Character	Passive	Stagnation	Walking on the Edge

Trigram	⚌ (Tui)	⚌ (Ch'ien)
Chinese Name	Tui	Ch'ien
Name	Lake	Heaven
Adjective	The Joyous	The Creative
Relationship	Yang/Yang/Yin	All Yang
Element	Metal	Metal
Status	Youngest Daughter	Father
Direction	West	North-West
Number	7	6
Life Area	Serenity	Creation
Area in Family Life	Children	Central Supporting Man
Behavioral Characteristic	Substance	Enlightenment
Seasons	Fall	End of Summer
Time of Day	Evening	Beginning of Night
Animal World	Sheep	Horse
Man's Body	Mouth	Head
Color	Blue	Purple
Symbol	Lake	Heaven
Character	Joy	Creation

This table, which summarizes all the concepts, is the most accepted one.

The order of trigrams appears in the *pah kwa*, a drawing that is a significant tool of Feng Shui, serving as a charm which, according to Chinese belief, protects, by means of its beautiful, colorful shape, against negative energies in general and death (or poison) arrows (*shar chi*) in particular. The pah kwa may be found, for example, at the centre of the "compass," which will be dealt with later on. Thus, a mirror with a pah kwa-shaped frame is a common and powerful Feng Shui tool, used to alter the flow of negative energy. Usually the pah kwa appears with the t'ai chi symbol (yin/yang) at its center, surrounded by the eight trigrams which are arranged according to their respective directions, and each is marked by its characteristic color.

There are two kinds of pah kwa drawings that can be purchased:

Yin pah kwa, also known as "Earlier Heaven," which is used mostly in regard to the location and direction of graves. The Chinese strongly believe that ancestral tombs exert a great influence on destiny and good fortune, and consequently their location (or shape) is sometimes of greater importance than the location of houses. This pah kwa is more widespread in Eastern countries than in the West, despite its importance.

Yang pah kwa, also known as "Later Heaven," which is used mostly in regard to the location and direction of buildings for the living. This is the accepted and widespread use of pah kwa in Western countries.

The directions are identical in both forms of pah kwa (the south always appears at the top, as the Chinese believe it is the beginning of all things and give it its due respect); however, the order of trigrams and their association with the directions are different:

DIRECTION	YIN PAH KWA	YANG PAH KWA
South	☰	☷
South-West	☱	☶
West	☲	☵
North-West	☳	☴
North	☷	☰
North-East	☶	☱
East	☵	☲
South-East	☴	☳

The elements

The five elements are a significant part of Chinese philosophy and Feng Shui, as well as the relations between them, which may be either constructive or destructive, and in turn lead to the creation of cycles of "creation" or "destruction."

Let us examine the elements from the point of view of Feng Shui, that is, in terms of the energy flow of each element, and sum it all up in a chart.

The world is composed of the following elements:

Fire: Energy which shoots upward (like the flame itself). It comes to full expression when one is at the peak of life. It is summer. Having reached its climax, the fire begins to fade and soon it will disappear and seek rest.

Earth: Energy which moves horizontally around its own axis. It is manifested during changes of seasons. Sometimes it is shown as a point at the center of the cycle of energy, representing a phase between the upward flowing energy of fire and the inward flowing energy of metal.

Metal: A "dense" energy (due to its mass), which flows inward. It has concentrated, dense qualities. (The Chinese call this "energy that tends to coagulate," like blood.) It is fall.

Water: Energy which flows downward, representing the point of maximum rest during the cycle of life; therefore, this energy is essential and concentrated. It is winter.

Wood: A powerful energy which flows outward in all directions, just like a tree growing out of its seed. This is the phase of growth during the life cycle, the most important. It is spring.

The five elements interact within two systems:

1. **The mother-child system:** This is the creative cycle in which each element functions as the parent, or creator, of another element, and at the same time serves as the child, or creation, of another element, thus forming a creative cycle.

2. **The control system:** This is the destructive system in which each element is capable of destroying another element (and therefore controls it), and may at the same time be destroyed by another element (by which it is controlled), thus forming a cycle of control.

The two systems, or cycles, are graphically depicted as follows:

The cycle of creation:

Wood creates fire.

Fire creates earth.

Earth creates metal.

Metal creates water.

Water creates wood.

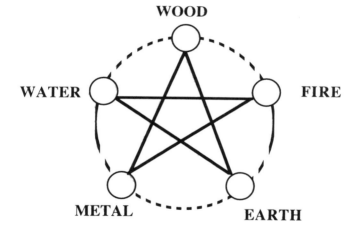

The cycle of control:

Wood destroys earth.
Earth destroys water.
Water destroys fire.
Fire destroys metal.
Metal destroys wood.

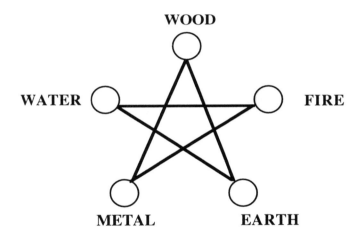

The following chart presents the full meaning of each element:

	Fire	Earth	Metal	Water	Wood
Star	Mars	Saturn	Venus	Mercury	Jupiter
Color	Red	Yellow	White	Black	Green
Taste	Bitter	Sweet	Acid	Salty	Sour
Type of Animal	Birds	Humans	Mammals	Shellfish	Fish
Yin/Yang	Big Yang	Equal	Less Yin	Big Yin	Less Yang
Direction	South	South-West North-East	West North-West	North	East South-East
In Harmony	Earth	Metal	Water	Wood	Fire
In Contrast	Metal	Water	Wood	Fire	Earth

Lo Shuh - the magic square

The magic square, or number box, is a significant concept in all Chinese mystical theories, including Feng Shui. It consists of nine squares, with a number in each square. The sum of the three squares in every direction - horizontally, vertically or diagonally - is always 15.

The magic square is used mostly to understand the space where Feng Shui operates, as well as the time factor in that space. The borders of the middle square, which contains the number 5, are all shared with other squares; it represents the center of t'ai-chi, which we have already discussed, and the snake, which will be discussed later on. Theoretically speaking, this square is located at the center of the *lo pan*, which is the main practical tool of Feng Shui, and will be discussed shortly. The eight remaining squares represent the eight directions according to Chinese philosophy, while each number is also associated with a trigram that lies in the same direction. We shall see that every person is represented by one of the eight figures, which is calculated according to the numbers constituting the Chinese date of birth.

In ancient China, the wise men used tortoiseshell for predicting the future: They would drill a hole in the shell and then throw it into the fire. The flame would crack the shell and the future could be divined through the pattern of the cracks. According to tradition, the linear system of future divination (broken or solid lines) which appears in the *I Ching* originated from this method.

According to tradition, the legendary Emperor Yu one day came upon a tortoise climbing out of the river Lo. The tortoise had the magic square carved on its shell, with each number represented by circles which were joined together by a thread. Emperor Yu realized this was a sign, and became the first to make rules based on the magic square, lo shuh. This is why ancient Chinese towns were divided into nine divisions, each one distinguished according to its unique number. A similar division may be found in palaces, temples, symbolic paintings, etc.

Lo shuh looks like this:

4	9	2
3	5	7
8	1	6

The shape of lo shuh - more precisely, the location of the numbers in the square, is crucial to determining the nature of a person's year of birth. Every year has its own particular nature, determined by the dominant number or by the direction associated with that year. We shall later see how the magic square determines the nature of the year, but first we must get acquainted with the Chinese calendar and see how it is used to figure out a person's personal number which, in turn, determines his character (just like the nature of the year).

The Chinese calendar

The Chinese calendar is by nature far more comprehensive than the Western calendar, particularly regarding Feng Shui. In addition to the date, the calendar also lists the directions from which positive energy flows on each day and on each part of the day. Thus, if you start building a house on a particular day, you can learn from the calendar in what direction to work on that day.

The Chinese calendar also advises what should or should not be done on a particular day, and describes the position of the stars, the state of the elements, etc. In terms of Feng Shui, however, the greatest importance of the Chinese calendar lies in the possibility of figuring out the personal number, known as the *kwa* number, and finding the dominant element of each year.

As this book is directed at people from Western cultures, let us try and match the Chinese calendar with the Western one. The Chinese year starts in the first week of February. Someone who was born on January 20th, 1960 is considered by the Chinese to have been born in 1959.

Further difficulties arise from the fact that various methods are used to convert Chinese calendar into the Western one. Certain charts, for instance, show February 2nd as the first day of 1946, whereas others determine that February 4th was the first day of that year. We recommend, as a rule, to mark February 5th as the first day of the Chinese year: According to the Western calendar, the year of birth of anyone who was born between January 1st and February 4th is the same as the year of birth of someone who was born on February 5th, whereas according to the Chinese calendar, he was born the previous year. (An accurate chart is included in the Appendix, but it is important to note that there are other charts which are based on slightly different methods of calculation.)

Let us now figure out the kwa, or personal, number. The number can be calculated in two possible ways, but the method of calculation is different for men and for women.

According to a person's year of birth, as it appears in the Chinese calendar:

For men: Add the last two digits of the year of birth according to the Chinese calendar and reduce them (as you would in Numerology) until you end up with one digit. When you subtract it from 10, you get the man's kwa number. (If the year in question is 1900, then the sum is 10-0 = 10, which you then reduce to 1.)

If the difference is 5, the man's personal kwa number will be 2.

For example: The year of birth is 1975.

7+5 = 12 = 1+2 = 3. Then 10-3=7;

7 is the kwa number.

For women: Add the last two digits of the year of birth according to the Chinese calendar and reduce them (as you would in Numerology) until you end up with one digit. Add 5 to the sum, reduce it to one digit, and you have the woman's kwa number.

If the result is 5, the woman's personal kwa number will be 8.

For example: The year of birth is 1975.

$7+5 = 12 = 1+2 = 3$. Then $3+5 = 8$;

8 is the kwa number.

According to the principle of dividing by nine:

For men: Subtract the last two digits of the year of birth as it appears in the Chinese calendar from 100 and divide the difference by 9. The remainder is the man's personal kwa number.

If there is no remainder, the kwa number is 9.

If the quotient is 5, the kwa number is 2.

For example: The year of birth is 1975. $100-75 = 25$. 25 divided by 9 equals 2 remainder 7; 7 is the kwa number.

For women: Subtract 4 from the last two digits of the year of birth and divide the difference by 9. The remainder is the woman's personal kwa number.

If there is no remainder, the kwa number is 9.

If the quotient is 5, the kwa number is 8.

For example: The year of birth is 1975. $75-4 = 71$. 71 divided by 9 equals 7 remainder 8; 8 is the kwa number.

The personal number allows us to distinguish between two groups of people: "east-oriented" and "west-oriented," or Easterners and Westerners. Each group contains four sub-groups, according to the personal numbers. Each sub-group has its own personal kwa "compass" consisting of the eight accepted directions, four of which are positive and four negative in terms of energy flow. Normally, a precise description of the kind of energy involved - either positive or negative - is attached to each direction. In other words, this is a personal compass which applies the principles of Feng Shui to the individual.

The group of Easterners includes the numbers
1, 3, 4, 9.
The group of Westerners includes the numbers
2, 6, 7, 8.

The division of kwa directions into positive and negative, according to the personal number.

EAST PEOPLE

South-East   South

4	9	2
3	5	7
8	1	6

East (row 2, left)

North

WEST PEOPLE

South-West (top right)

4	9	2
3	5	7
8	1	6

West (row 2, right)

North-East (bottom left)   North-West (bottom right)

In order to receive an explanation, we will now go on to the next topic, *ki*, and there we will present the meaning of the eight "compasses."

Ki -
the number of the year

Each year of the Chinese calendar has its own individual number as well as its own "compass." The "compass" consists of eight directions and nine numbers: the number at the center, which is the personal number of the year, and eight additional numbers which represent the eight directions. Thus, each year has many attributes which are associated with number and direction.

Every ki is named after its central number, and all eight ki compasses are arranged according to the order of the magic square known as *lo shuh.* The central "compass" or "the compass of number 5" is also known as "the ki ruler," as it is the standard against which all the other numbers are checked.

Ki enables us to find out the traits associated with each year and in turn allows us to combine this knowledge with the information provided by the kwa compass mentioned above.

The appendix at the end of the book includes the ki numbers of each year according to the Chinese calendar. The method of calculation is very simple, as you only need to know the ki number of one year (for example, the year of your birth) in order to find the ki number of every other year.

Note: In traditional Chinese writings, the direction "South" usually appears at the top of the page, facing upward. The charts included in this book are arranged according to the Chinese method. Although this is not a crucial matter, it is advisable to check the location of North/South in advance whenever you use other books or calendars.

The table for the number five compass looks like this:

South	9
South-East	4
East	3
North-East	8
North	1
North-West	6
West	7
South-West	2

South-East ↖ South | ↗ South-West

East — 3 —(5)— 7 — West

North-East ↙ 8 North 1 ↘ 6 North-West

(The basic characteristics of the different directions can be found in the detailed table.)

The eight ki "compasses" look like this:
The compasses of Easterners are 1, 3, 4 and 9.

Ki number 1

South	5	Longevity
South-East	9	Vitality
East	8	Good Luck
North-East	4	Distress
North	6	Life
North-West	2	Powerful Enemy
West	3	Disaster
South-West	7	Death

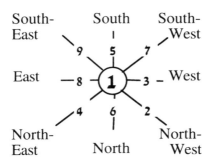

Ki number 3

South	7	Vitality
South-East	2	Longevity
East	1	Life
North-East	6	Powerful Enemy
North	8	Good Luck
North-West	4	Distress
West	5	Death
South-West	9	Disaster

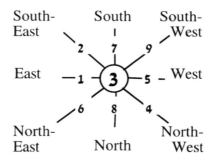

Ki number 4

South	8	Good Luck
South-East	3	Life
East	2	Longevity
North-East	7	Death
North	9	Vitality
North-West	5	Disaster
West	6	Powerful Enemy
South-West	1	Distress

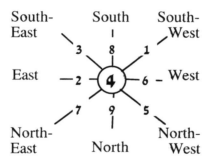

Ki number 9

South	4	Life
South-East	8	Good Luck
East	7	Vitality
North-East	3	Disaster
North	5	Longevity
North-West	1	Death
West	2	Distress
South-West	6	Powerful Enemy

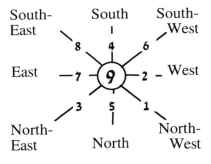

The compasses of Westerners are 2, 6, 7 and 8.

Ki number 2

South	6	Powerful Enemy
South-East	1	Distress
East	9	Disaster
North-East	5	Vitality
North	7	Death
North-West	3	Longevity
West	4	Good Luck
South-West	8	Life

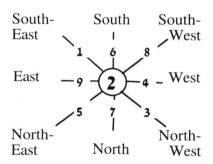

Ki number 6

South	1	Death
South-East	5	Disaster
East	4	Distress
North-East	9	Good Luck
North	2	Powerful Enemy
North-West	7	Life
West	8	Vitality
South-West	3	Longevity

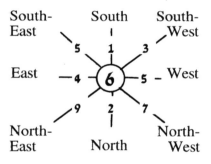

Ki number 7

South	2	Distress
South-East	6	Powerful Enemy
East	5	Death
North-East	1	Longevity
North	3	Disaster
North-West	8	Vitality
West	9	Life
South-West	4	Good Luck

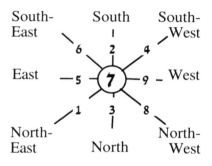

Ki number 8

South	3	Disaster
South-East	7	Death
East	6	Powerful Enemy
North-East	2	Life
North	4	Distress
North-West	9	Good Luck
West	1	Longevity
South-West	5	Vitality

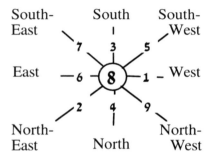

That is, a number 8 person (who belongs to "West" people) who desires longevity will ensure that the entrance to his house faces west. A number 3 person (who belongs to "East" people) who desires longevity will ensure that the entrance to his house faces south-east. The entrance of a new house which was begun in a number 6 year must not face south, since this will bring death to its inhabitants.

Ki compasses are the principal tools of the Feng Shui Master, and utilizing them demands knowledge, skill and experience.

Year cycles

According to Chinese philosophy, everything in the universe, including the concept of time, is based on certain cyclical patterns: day and night, the seasons of the year, or the cycles of the years.

Year cycles are determined according to the five elements. Consequently, each year is linked with a single element which is, in fact, its "birth mark." The year in question is dominated by that one element, so that we can refer to it, for example, as a "metallic" or "wooden" year. This, combined with a person's exact date of birth according to the Chinese calendar, is a crucial factor in determining the directions of that person's house.

According to the Chinese calendar, every two years are dominated by a single element, whereas the cycle itself is renewed every ten years.

All you have to do is to find your year of birth according to the Chinese calendar and remember its dominant element.

The five elements in the calendar

wood	fire	earth	metal	water
1904	1906	1908	1900	1902
1905	1907	1909	1901	1903
1914	1916	1918	1910	1912
1915	1917	1919	1911	1913
1924	1926	1928	1920	1922
1925	1927	1929	1921	1923
1934	1936	1938	1930	1932
1935	1937	1939	1931	1933
1944	1946	1948	1940	1942
1945	1947	1949	1941	1943
1954	1956	1958	1950	1952
1955	1957	1959	1951	1953
1964	1966	1968	1960	1962
1965	1967	1969	1961	1963
1974	1976	1978	1970	1972
1975	1977	1979	1971	1973
1984	1986	1988	1980	1982
1985	1987	1989	1981	1983
1994	1996	1998	1990	1992
1995	1997	1999	1991	1993
2004	2006	2008	2000	2002
2005	2007	2009	2001	2003
2014	2016	2018	2010	2012

And so on.

Feng Shui rulers

In addition to the directions which determine the flow of energy, the size and proportions of every object are extremely significant. Each object, large or small, has measurements of its own, whether it is a table, a bed, a window, a sheet of writing paper, and so on. Each measurement has good or bad qualities attached to it. Thus, a seven-centimeter-high bed can cause severe illness, whereas a 24-centimeter-long notebook guarantees success in exams.

Feng Shui rulers are used in order to ensure that all things are properly sized.

The most common ruler, which is 87 centimeters (34 inches) long, is divided into eight sections: Four have a positive influence and four have a negative one. Each section may normally be further divided into four or eight sub-sections.

The following sections possess good qualities:

Good luck			Powerful friend	Strength			Wealth
1	2	3	4	5	6	7	8

The following sections possess negative traits:

	Illness	Bad luck			Loss	Disaster	
1	2	3	4	5	6	7	8

When you measure an object which is more than 87 centimeters long, the sections repeat themselves all over again.

It is recommended for anyone wishing to enjoy the full advantages of Feng Shui to prepare a proper wooden ruler with the various sections marked on it (in different colors).

The Feng Shui Masters use a second ruler, which is known as "the 8/10 or 32/40 ruler." Although it is normally one meter or about 40" long, it also exists in different sizes.

Significantly, this ruler - which is used in addition to the common ruler - is divided on one side into ten identical sections, and on the other side into eight sections. Each of the sections on both sides is in turn divided into four sub-sections. The division is from 0 up to 100 centimeters, which means that on one side there are 10 sections of 10 centimeters each, and on the other, eight sections of 12.5 centimeters each. Each section is further divided into four sub-sections. Therefore, in addition to measurements (either centimeters or inches), this ruler contains Feng Shui instructions in the form of sections.

The side which contains a total of 40 sub-sections is used to take **interior** measures of objects, utensils, or parts of the house. Every section carries with it a positive or negative energy, as defined by the four sub-sections. After taking the interior measurements of the object, you can see into which of the 40 sub-sections it fits, and understand the Feng Shui associated with this particular measure.

The ten sections used to take interior measurements are as follows:

1-4	Damage
5-8	Prosperity
9-12	Disaster
13-16	Reason
17-20	Honor
21-24	Death
25-28	Expansion
29-32	Loss
33-36	Wealth
37-40	Fertility

Similarly, the side which contains eight sections, or 32 sub-sections, is used for taking various **exterior** measurements.

The eight sections used for taking exterior measurements are as follows:

1-4	Wealth
5-8	Illness
9-12	Separation
13-16	Reason
17-20	Title
21-24	Robbery
25-28	Damage
29-32	Assets

Lo Pan -
the Feng Shui "compass"

A useful tool of Feng Shui is the "compass" known as *lo pan*. In fact, lo pan is more of an advanced calculation implement upon which all the Feng Shui formulas are written, rather than an ordinary compass in the Western sense.

The lo pan is a circular ruler, with a smaller circle (representing t'ai chi, which is the center where everything begins) located at its center. The 360 degrees are divided into eight sections, some of which are further divided into sub-sections. There are concentric rings which radiate outward from the t'ai chi. There might be up to forty rings in an advanced lo pan, representing all things in the universe, from directions and planetary movements to the angles of the sunrise, the 64 hexagrams of the *I Ching*, and the dozen halls which are linked with the twelve "dead."

Lo pan in fact holds together the essential information used by the Feng Shui Master. Standing at the site about to be examined, the Master places the lo pan horizontally. The Master then uses the magnetic compass located at the center of lo pan (t'ai chi) to find the North (or, rather, the South which is the first direction in China), turning the lo pan until the cross at its center is aligned with the North/South axis as indicated by the magnetic compass. The Master may find all the information he needs in order to practice Feng Shui along the line which comes out of the center of lo pan in the direction of his gaze .

The traditional lo pan does not include the directions (which are determined by the compass). The lo pan used by many Feng Shui masters today is similar in many ways to the traditional implement, except that it includes fewer rings, and the directions are indicated on it (so that if you know where the North is, you can align the lo pan without using a compass).

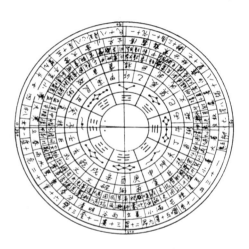

The traditional, as well as the modern lo pan, is divided into eight sections consisting of 45 degrees each, or 360 degrees in total. This is known as the lo pan of "equal division."

There is, however, a second traditional lo pan, used mostly in Feng Shui for determining the location of tombs, which is divided unequally: South, North, West and East are 30 degrees each, whereas South-East, South-West, North-West and North-East are 60 degrees each. This is known as the lo pan of "variable division."

Since the "variable" lo pan is not as unequivocal in its instructions as the "equal" one, it is regarded by Chinese philosophy as a more efficient means of compromising. Directions which unite two of the four points of the compass also combine traits which suit a broader range of people. Directions which include only a single point of the compass are more focused and suit a narrower range of people. Nevertheless, the "equal lo pan" is the more popular one.

Although experienced Masters have no need of the lo pan, they still tend to sketch its shape on a flat surface, such as a floor, a piece of paper, the ground or a wooden board. The South/North are usually indicated by an arrow, and the yin/yang symbol in the middle represents t'ai chi. The Master then draws a line in the direction of prominent objects such as mountains, towers, rivers, etc., noting down all the data he needs along the line. This leads to the creation of a special lo pan which suits the particular place and purpose for which the Feng Shui was performed (the construction of a house, the location of a tomb, business, love, etc.).

Since lo pan is merely an instrument, one may also use

a simple compass and detailed charts which list the meanings of the various directions and of the personal number, the number of the year, and so on. It is crucial to pick a particular direction and gather all the data concerning the flow of energy in that direction and its influences.

So far we have dealt with elements which stem from different directions. However, Feng Shui also takes into account the conditions of the terrain in the area under inspection. We shall now discuss this unique aspect of Feng Shui.

The two schools of Feng Shui

Chinese tradition recognizes two schools of Feng Shui: the first, which deals mostly with directions and employs the lo pan, and the second, which is based on the conditions of the terrain and uses the "animal map" described below. Nowadays, Masters who practice Feng Shui tend to combine the two methods.

The "animal map" of Feng Shui

One of the main tools of Feng Shui is a graphic, multifaceted, ever-changing map which is unique to every human being or structure. In addition to these advantages, the map consists of four directions and a center, each possessing specific traits of its own.

Significantly, the map is created by the person or structure under the inspection of the Feng Shui Master. If, for instance, you wish to design a Feng Shui map for your house, all you have to do is to stand at the door and look outside, and you have already created the "animal map."

The direction in which you are facing when standing at the door is defined in the animal map as the **phoenix** or "yellow bird."

The direction behind you is the **tortoise**.

The direction on your right is the **tiger**.

The direction on your left is the **dragon**.

You are standing at the center, which is known as the **"coiled snake."**

Let us assume that you decide to make renovations, brick up the front door and move the main entrance to the back of the house. Once the work is complete and you stand at the door:

The phoenix is opposite you (where the tortoise was before).

The tortoise is behind you (where the phoenix was before).

The tiger is on your right (where the dragon was before).

The dragon is on your left (where the tiger was before).

You are at the center, which is known as the "coiled snake."

In other words, the starting point for this map and the most significant element in it is the direction in which the person (or the front of the house, or the front of the tomb) is facing, as the whole map is built around it.

Naturally, certain directions are more favorable than others, as they match the points of the compass. The phoenix should be positioned in the south. The tortoise should be positioned in the north. The tiger should be in the west. The dragon should be in the east. The coiled snake will always be at the center.

According to Chinese philosophy, there are desirable traits and characteristic areas for each of the animals.

The **phoenix,** at the front, is positioned in the south, its color is red, its season is summer, and its element is fire.

The phoenix is a mythical bird which is consumed by fire and then rises again from the flames. That is, it never really dies. It represents our capacity for vision, always looking ahead (or, in other words, looking into the future). In Feng Shui, the phoenix represents our capacity to watch and learn, or the senses which allow us to merge with our surroundings.

Once the phoenix fully complies with the rules of Feng Shui - when, for example, the door faces south, opposite a red object and a source of light (fire) - then it is assured that the senses are at their utmost alertness and that complete harmony with nature will be achieved.

The **tortoise**, at the back, is positioned in the north, its color is black, its season is winter, and its element is water.

The tortoise is characterized by its protective shell, its stability and defensive capabilities. It is mostly associated with providing protection and safety, and with the ability to guard the rear. A tortoise complying with the rules of Feng Shui provides protection and great security, guarding against danger coming from the rear.

The **tiger,** on the right, is situated in the west, its color is white, its season is fall, and its element is metal.

The tiger is a predator, fast and violent, quite capable of attacking its assailants, proving that attack is sometimes the best possible defense. This capacity is crucial for survival (but it can also drag the tiger into undesirable situations). According to Feng Shui, the tiger is forever on the alert, always ready to attack. (It is important to remember, though, that violence might be dangerous, so the tiger is "restrained" by the color white.) The tiger's position is of particular importance where tombs and buildings are concerned.

The **dragon,** on the left, is positioned in the east, its color is green, its season is spring, and its element is wood.

Like the phoenix, the dragon is a mythical creature, marked by its capacity to fly and to see into the distance, far beyond the scope of the human eye. According to Feng Shui, the dragon absorbs information gathered by the senses (aided by the phoenix) and, inspired by the details, guides man on his way. Since the dragon soars high above solid ground, it mainly influences the mind and the spirit. You can only be enlightened spiritually if you position the dragon in a favorable place. The dragon is particularly important for the location of temples and shrines.

The **snake**, in the middle (like the t'ai chi), is yellow-brown like the color of the earth, and is also at the center of the changing seasons.

The snake, coiled on the ground, is protected by the four surrounding animals which, at the same time, all respond to its movement. That is, the snake is just like the head which operates the various parts, creates communication between them, and balances them against one another.

The terrain

Feng Shui uses the terrain as a yardstick and, according to Chinese tradition, deals mostly with the effect of two elements: hills or mountains, and water currents. One should bear in mind that Feng Shui evolved in a rural, agricultural society where the natural terrain was of the utmost importance. In the modern world, one must relate to a man-made environment similarly. Highways and railways, for example, which serve as a means of transportation and mobility, are similar in function to the rivers of days gone by, and may therefore be analyzed in a similar manner. Although big buildings, walls and various structures are man-made, they are related to just like hills.

The two basic groups are "hills," representing the shape of the ground, and "rivers," representing the shape of the water line. Each of the five basic shapes is associated with one of the elements.

The person seeking the help of Feng Shui was born in a year which is also associated with a certain element, so that the Master's principal task is to find a match between the person's "personal" element and the element linked with the shape of the ground (and eventually to insert this detail into the general Feng Shui map). Hence, we need to go back to the two element cycles: that of creation and that of control (or destruction).

The basic rule is this: A person should always aspire for his house to be influenced by a "parent" element, and stay away from an element which might control (and therefore destroy) it.

For example, a person whose element is fire should build his house near a ground shape which contains the element of wood, but should stay away from ground shapes which contain the water element.

The **Hill of Fire**, which is high and pointed, with triangular cliffs, is good for people whose element is earth and bad for people whose element is metal. (When the Hill of Fire is situated in front of the house, though, it sends a "death arrow" which exerts a negative influence.)

The **Hill of Wood,** which is high and round, with several peaks reminiscent of rounded fingers, is good for people whose element is fire and bad for people whose element is earth. (When it is situated at the back of the house, it becomes a perfect "tortoise" and therefore exerts a positive influence.)

The **Hill of Earth** is low and round, not unlike an overturned plate. It is good for people whose element is metal and bad for people whose element is water.

The **Hill of Metal** is small and round and looks like cookies on a plate. It is good for people whose element is water and bad for people whose element is wood.

The **Hill of Water,** which is pointed, low (with no sharp cliffs) and spread outward, is good for people whose element is wood and bad for people whose element is fire.

The water ways are similarly analyzed. Like the hills, they are also divided into five elements, and these shapes are either good or bad for people associated with the various elements.

The **River of Fire** has an acute-angled curve.

The **River of Wood** has an obtuse-angled curve.

The **River of Earth** is marked by two consecutive curves which, turning in opposite directions, create the shape of a 2 or an S.

The **River of Metal** has an acute-angled curve but the angle itself is rounded.

The **River of Water** has moderate but consecutive curves, rather like a coil.

All this may be summed up in the following chart:

Element

hill	fire	wood	earth	metal	water
good for	earth	fire	metal	water	wood
bad for	metal	earth	water	wood	fire

Element

river	fire	wood	earth	metal	water
good for	earth	fire	metal	water	wood
bad for	metal	earth	water	wood	fire

The five shapes of Feng Shui

Feng Shui consists of five basic shapes, each having its own attributes and links with the elements of Feng Shui. Each shape, as we shall see, largely affects the accumulation and flow of energy (chi) in its surroundings.

The **square**, associated with the element of earth, by nature represents security, stability, support and a certain "square" quality. It is also associated with the yellowish-brown colors of the earth. This shape is suitable for human dwellings.

The flowing energy encounters the front of the square shape and accumulates in the form of a whirlpool or energy circle in front of the structure.

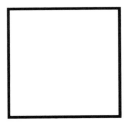

The **triangle**, associated with the element of fire, by nature points upward to the sky. It represents the aspiration for enlightenment, to "soar" and reach a higher level. It is associated with red or reddish-yellow (being a combination of fire and sun). This shape is particularly suitable for tombs or places of religious activity (such as temples and pagodas).

When the flowing energy encounters the sloping sides of the triangle, it climbs upward to the pillar of energy hovering above the apex of the triangle.

The **vertical rectangle**, associated with the element of wood and representing growth and development by nature, is a powerful and influential shape. It is associated with green. This shape is particularly suitable for business purposes.

The flowing energy encounters the structure and creates a powerful ball of energy which, being adjacent to the structure, may either gnaw at it or strengthen it.

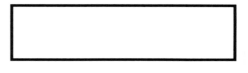

The **horizontal rectangle**, associated with the water element (usually a curving rather than a perfect rectangle), is by nature a flowing shape, particularly regarding the surrounding landscape. It represents adjustment, flowing and consistency.

It is associated with deep blue and, according to various schools, with black, too. It is particularly suitable for state buildings, educational and cultural institutions, and so on.

The flowing energy encounters the front of the building, streams along its front and merges with its shape.

The **round shape**, associated with the element of metal, represents force and concentrated force. Unlike the other shapes, the flowing energy accumulates at the center of the round shape, for example, in the hollow of the tower. This shape is associated with white and is mainly suitable for military installations (watch-towers) or symbolic structures (obelisks, bell towers, etc).

Having encountered the round structure from all directions, the flowing energy penetrates it (there is an elongated shaft at the center of the structure), and it can then move upward or downward (like a chimney).

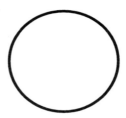

Flawed shapes

Feng Shui regards all flawed shapes as a source of trouble. The triangle, for example, is considered a source of negative energy since it is, in fact, a flawed shape created by splitting the square or the rectangle. When the triangle is flawed, its negative influence grows stronger. The principle of preserving the wholeness of the basic shapes is of the utmost importance to designing houses, furniture and everyday objects, as well as to planning cities, dividing up agricultural plots and so on.

Once you practice Feng Shui, you will have to find the direction of the t'ai-chi, or the middle point of the compass used by the Master, which is usually located at the center of the room. Finding the center point is quite easy if you are dealing with a basic, complete shape. It is much harder if the shape is flawed. (In that case you have to sub-divide the flawed shape, find the center point of each part, and then examine each one separately.) A warning: Never attempt to complete the flawed shape by "filling it in."

Flawed shapes might look like this:

In the case of an L-shaped house, for example, it is very difficult to find the center, so the middle point of each wing must be calculated separately. It is forbidden to complete the shape into a " Ⅱ" so as to find a single center point.

Death arrows, or Shar Chi

The natural inclination of Feng Shui is to regard the flow of chi, or energy, as a positive phenomenon. This flow of energy might be impaired by certain terrain conditions or incompatibilities between man and the environment, so that the Feng Shui Master must fix the damage and put the flow back on track.

However, certain terrain conditions - either natural or man-made - are inclined by nature to invoke negative energy flow. This energy, known as *shar chi*, is liable to originate from any direction in which a certain structure is facing, but it is much more powerful if it flows into the front or entrance of the structure. This negative energy, known as "death arrow," must be avoided, as it can also prove to be lethal.

There are three basic shapes which might create death arrows:

1. A straight line running along a relatively long distance - such as a straight road, a straight row of trees, etc.

2. An acute angle or triangle - such as a sharp corner in a building, a sloping roof which creates an arrowhead, a piece of land in the shape of an elongated triangle, etc.

3. An element which used to be alive but now has no life (and has not been properly buried or "disposed of"), such as a dead tree trunk, a demolished house, a withered garden, etc.

As mentioned above, the influence of the death arrows is especially powerful if they point toward the front of the house or the tomb - so strong that a single arrow can destroy the positive influence of the tiger, the dragon and the tortoise. (The phoenix, in fact, becomes the source of evil, since it is located at the front, and the shar chi resides in it.)

In man's natural environment, death arrows are usually caused by straight or triangular structures or conditions of terrain which pose a threat to houses or tombs. These arrows are sometimes visible, but they are sometimes concealed, in which case only the Master can discover them.

Upon first surveying the area, the Feng Shui Master tries to locate possible causes for death arrows: triangular roofs, a long straight fence, a sharp corner of a building, a straight part of a river, a tower with a triangular roof, an intersection, etc.

According to Wang Tann, triangular roofs are the major cause of death arrows, followed by straight roads and highways, crossroads (particularly modern junctions or interchanges), tall towers, and finally high, jagged mountains and hills. As mentioned before, shar chi sources which are located opposite the front of the house have an extremely negative influence!

It is important to remember that shar chi exists not only outside, but also inside the house, and although the influence of death arrows is much weaker here, it is evident in large and small objects and their arrangement.

Fortunately, as we shall learn later from various examples, Feng Shui employs a highly efficient, clever method of altering the flow of negative energy and protecting against it, based on relatively simple means, such as mirrors, mobiles, pah kwa drawings, screens, curtains, flowerpots, and lamps for altering lighting conditions.

"Rules of thumb" of Feng Shui

Put simply, Feng Shui has three aims:
Harmony with the environment.
Balance in life.
Blending with the natural environment.

In order to achieve these aims, three rules of thumb must be followed:
A "mountain" behind.
Open ground in front.
A surface of water within the range of vision.

If these principles are adhered to, then the Feng Shui is likely to be positive.

Excess

The term "excess" refers to an excess of yin or yang, which is caused by the natural state of things rather than by blockages or accidents. As far as Feng Shui is concerned, a house or a structure may have an excess of either yin or yang.

An **excess of yin** is created when the house is located next to a place which is dominated by death (a cemetery, a hospital, a butcher's shop, a lumber yard, etc.).

It is also created by places which are associated with death, such as cenotaphs, monuments or shrines. An excess of yin which originates from a structure built on "dead" ground, such as an old cemetery, is particularly dangerous. There is also an excess of yin in dark, damp, poorly maintained structures, or in buildings which were occupied by terminally ill people.

When there is an excess of yin, it is advisable to keep the front door of the structure, as well as other openings, away from the yin source (a cemetery, for example). The structure must be painted light red. It must be full of light (during the night, too, if possible), and sources of darkness or shadow should be eliminated. Flower-beds are better than trees or tall plants. There should be a paved area rather than a lawn in front of the house, and, above all - the roof must be red.

An **excess of yang** is created if the house is near to a source of heat or concentrated energy (factories, high voltage lines and so on). Structures in hot, bright environments (a desert, for example) also suffer from an excess of yang. Even structures which are exposed to sunlight during most of the day and are subject to loud noise and strong sound reverberation suffer from an excess of yang.

In the case of an excess of yang, it is advisable to move the door and openings of the house away from the yang source and to let the color blue predominate. The quieter the house, the stronger the balancing influence of the yin. Excessive light should be avoided, and under no circumstances must light pass through a red filter (such as a red screen), as it can become truly dangerous. Water sources such as fountains, fish-ponds or paintings of lakes, are beneficial. A green lawn with spots of black will also help.

In short, problems of an excess of yin necessitate an intensified presence of yang, whereas problems of an excess of yang necessitate an intensified presence of yin.

Ten pieces of advice for living in an environment with an excess of yang

1. Place water surfaces such as small ponds, fountains, aquariums or round water jars inside the house, particularly at the entrance.

2. Use blue paint, particularly on the doors and windows. Plant blue flowers in the garden and in the flowerpots.

3. Use dim lighting and avoid over-exposure to the sun or to direct light. Light sources should be concealed rather than visible. Do not use colored lamps (especially not red lamps).

4. Use natural-colored timber for the walls and fences. Surfaces (especially metal ones) may be painted black.

5. Make sure that silence is preserved and that there are noise-absorbing elements, such as carpets or curtains, in the house. In case of an external source of noise, the structure must be insulated. Perpetual noise is a dangerous enemy.

6. A flat lawn in front of the house is always helpful.

7. Hang paintings which contain green-blue colors (and particularly water motifs) on the walls of the house, especially at the entrance.

8. Avoid incessant movement of objects in and around the house. For example, it is not advisable to hang a mobile at the entrance of the house, since its motion increases the yang level.

9. If you spot the yang source, place a fountain or a small pond between the source and the house.

10. Keep the windows and doors of the house closed in order to prevent the yang from penetrating inside, since wide openings in the walls of the structure are liable to make the yang stronger.

Ten pieces of advice for living in an environment with an excess of yin

1. Place **yang** surfaces all over the house, especially at the entrance. These may include, for instance, boulders, pebble or stone surfaces, a cobbled path (preferably winding), etc.

2. Use red paint, particularly on chimneys, window and door frames, the roof, and in the garden and flowerpots (either red flowers or plants with red leaves).

3. Use strong lighting and avoid dark corners. You must, for example, trim the branches of trees which shade the house so that light can penetrate, or use artificial light in shady places. Incidentally, the effect of light can be achieved by means of mirrors.

4. The outer part of the structure - the walls of the house and the fence - must be painted white or any other light color.

5. Try to let **direct**, bright sunlight into the house either through a wide window or through an opening in the roof. (You may use transparent roof tiles.)

6. A garden full of small trees and plants in front is useful.

7. There should be a red ornament or some kind of red surface at the front of the house, on the door or close to it.

8. Leave a light on at the entrance of the house 24 hours a day, even if it is only a small lamp or a candle.

9. If you spot the source of the yin excess, do not have any openings facing it. If possible, separate it from the house with a low fence.

10. Above all, if you spot the source of the yin excess, you must place the main opening of the house as far away from it as possible.

The chi (energy) flow

Although theoretically and philosophically speaking there are dozens of forms of energy flow, practically speaking there are only three forms: a straight flow, a coiled flow and a chaotic, "messy" flow.

A straight flow means that energy travels along a straight line, passing from one opening to the other. (The flow is considered straight even when it involves a turn to the right or left.) Although a straight line is the natural form of energy or chi flow, it must be remembered that any obstacle changes this flow either negatively or positively.

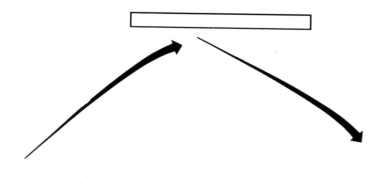

A coiled flow means that the advancing energy revolves around itself until it becomes a coil, so that in fact it creates the shape of a pipe rather than a line. In this case also, even when there is a turn, the form of the flow is more significant than its direction. A coiled flow is more powerful than a straight flow.

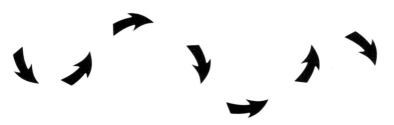

A chaotic flow, which is in fact a shapeless whirlpool of energy, is created when the flowing energy finds no opening to pass through or encounters a barrier or structures which compel it to twist in a manner which is inappropriate to the chi. The purpose of Feng Shui is in fact to prevent a chaotic flow.

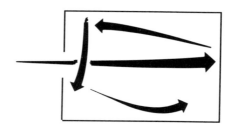

Arranging the rooms of the house

There are certain rules for the internal arrangement of the rooms in the house. Although each house must be examined separately according to its structure, there are a few rules of thumb which might prove helpful:

It is advisable to liken the inner division of the house to the division of the body: that is, the front door is similar to the mouth, whereas the back of the house is similar to the anus. Consequently, the kitchen should be located next to the entrance, while the bathrooms should be at the back of the house.

The bedroom should be at the center of the house.

In any case, the kitchen and the bathroom should be completely separate and as far away from each other as possible, depending on the structure of the house.

The proper location of the study is close to the front door, on the left.

The proper location of the living-room is close to the front door, on the right.

The direction of the bed

The bed we sleep in is one of the places in the house where we spend many hours. Although the location of the bed in the bedroom is extremely important, **the direction in which the head of the bed faces is just as significant.** This has been mentioned on several occasions throughout the book.

It must be remembered, though, that according to Feng Shui, each possible direction that the head of the bed can face has specific characteristics:

When the bed faces south, there is an excess of energy which prevents serene sleep. This direction is good for sex, but not for sleep.

When the bed faces north, there is a lack of energy which affords sound sleep, but is pretty boring. This direction is good for spiritual purposes. In Feng Shui this direction is known as "the gate of death" and is recommended for elderly people.

When the bed faces west, there is balanced energy, which affords sound sleep and a sense of satisfaction. This direction is suitable for people who do not feel the urge to act (that is, people who have already achieved their goals).

When the bed faces east, the direction is suitable for people who are at the beginning of the road. Sleep does not jeopardize the urge to act.

When the bed faces south-west (with the feet pointing toward the north-east), there is unstable energy, which can prove to be hazardous to the person.

When the bed faces south-east (with the feet pointing toward the north-west), there is a constructive kind of energy which reinforces the element of leadership and success in a person's life.

It must be noted, of course, that the direction of the head of the bed is merely one of many factors that determine the location of the bed, and that some of those factors are much more significant. The rule of thumb of Feng Shui determines that the bed should stand along the south-east/north-west axis in the innermost room of the house. Remember, too, that by learning the characteristics associated with the various directions, we may be able to solve problems which may occur in any direction.

The danger of the triangular plot of land

One of the most dangerous structures is the one that is built on a triangular plot of land, and even more so if it is a triangular structure on a triangular plot of land!

Let us assume, for example, that a square or rectangular structure is about to be built on a triangular plot of land.

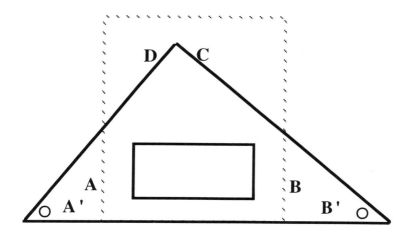

According to Feng Shui, great danger - possibly even sudden death - awaits the inhabitants of that house. First and foremost, therefore, we must solve the problem of the triangle.

To the best of our ability, wooden fences or hedges which will "break" the triangular plot and will make it as square as possible must be placed (A/B).

If the parts of the plot that have been separated are to be used, a pond or fountain must be put in front of the connecting gate (A'/B').

The triangle facing the door of the house must now be eliminated. This can be done by disposing of any fence or barrier which marks the triangular plot (parts C/D).

A wide lawn or paved surface will be placed in front of the house, with a winding path which will curve as much as possible to the right and left. This winding path is of the utmost importance.

There must be no form of tower, tall tree or pole in front of the house. The area which makes the modified plot into a square (the broken line) should be "cleared."

The mountain/pond balance

When there is a mountain, or a mountain-shaped structure, behind the house in the direction of the tortoise, a small pond or fountain may be built opposite the front door so that the path leading to the house will wind around one side of the pool. Such a combination assures good fortune.

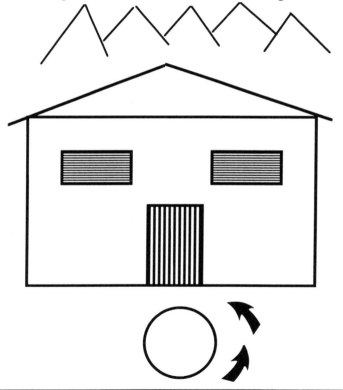

The danger of the tree

A tree located at the front of the house, particularly a "dying" tree, signifies bad luck. If the tree cannot be cut down or moved, the path leading to the house must make a wide detour and go around it.

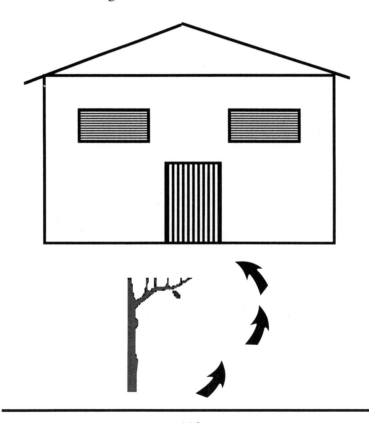

Using mirrors to correct flawed shapes

It is very common to use mirrors in order to correct flawed shapes, including ones that are "smaller" than they should be. The principles of use are relatively simple: Position a large mirror in such a way that the flawed shape is corrected by the reflection.

For example, in case of a flawed shape like this,

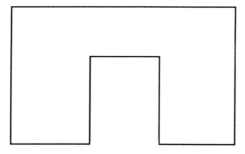

we must position the mirror on the part of the wall defined by the letter A, so that we end up with a reflection of the part created by the square AB:

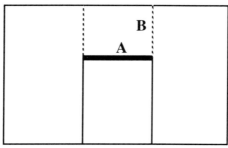

The reflection in the mirror will complete the shape through the virtual square AC.

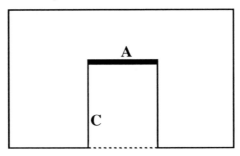

Another example: in the case of a flawed shape like this,

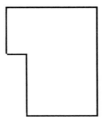

we must position the mirror on the part defined by the letter A, so that the reflection AB will complete the flawed shape.

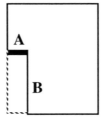

We use a mirror in order to correct the shape of a small room or a very narrow space in the house, preferably as close as possible to the shape of a square:

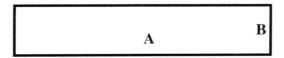

If we position a mirror on part A, the following shape will appear:

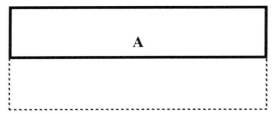

If, however, we position the mirror on part B, we shall end up with the following shape, which is not advisable:

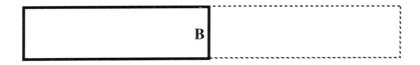

When we deal with a difficult structural shape, such as a corridor which is very long, it is possible that an undesirable "arrow" will be created by the straight, fast chi flow. We must therefore attempt to change the chi flow. We can achieve this without altering the shape of the structure by using mirrors.

For example: In the case of a corridor which is too long,

_____
_____   _____   _____   _____   _____   chi flow
_____

we must position mirrors along the bold lines so that the chi flow changes. **The mirrors must never face each other**.

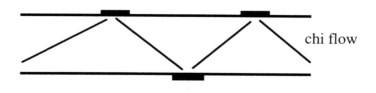

chi flow

We can implement the same principle if we have a vertical, ascending structure such as a flight of stairs. The mirrors must be placed so that they break the straight vertical motion of the chi flow:

What NOT to do in the bedroom

1. Never sleep with a mirror opposite the bed, as both the bed and its occupant/s are reflected in the mirror. It is therefore a negative factor.

The solution:

a. To remove the mirror.

b. To cover it with a curtain (or to place it inside a closet).

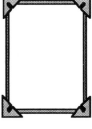

NO!

2. Never sleep with a television set, or another shiny object, opposite the bed, since the object serves as a mirror.

The solution:

Remove or cover it.

NO!

3. Never sleep in a bed that stands directly opposite the door of the room (especially if there is a window opposite the door). It is not a good position, no matter where the head of the bed is.

Solution:

The only thing possible is to move the bed.

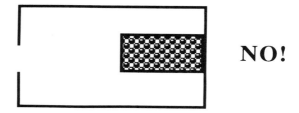

4. Never sleep with direct light (including direct light from a window) falling on the head of the bed.

Solution:

Curtains, lampshades, or refraction of the light on to the wall.

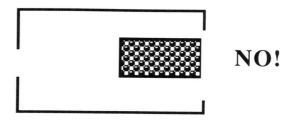

5. In the bedroom, there are always sharp angles (the corners, for example). Do not sleep with the head of the bed turned toward the angle. This is particularly serious when the room is neither square-shaped nor rectangular, but is cut off at some point.

Solution:

To push the head of the bed against one of the walls. (N.B. In this case, you may not use a mirror to correct the distortion in the room.)

Dead end

Many houses are built with paths leading to them, and the front entrance directly opposite the path. This is bad, as negative energy can flow into the house.

Solution:

Assuming that it is impossible to move the path, a wooden fence or hedge should be placed between the house and the path, and the entrance gate should be located as far as possible from the middle of the path, to the right or the left.

In addition, a little pond or fountain can be placed at the side of the path, or a small bush can be planted - preferably opposite the gate.

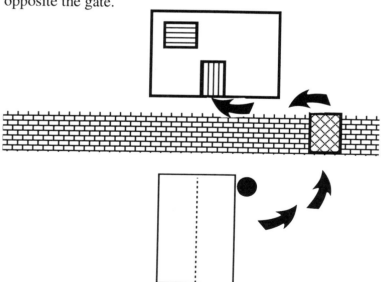

Internal staircases

When there are stairs inside a house, it is preferable that the door of a room, especially a bedroom, not be located directly opposite the staircase. If possible, the door should be moved so that someone going up the stairs will see a wall opposite him, and not a door. If this is not possible, a large vase containing water and flowers should be placed on a high narrow table near the door, or a round mirror should be hung on the wall.

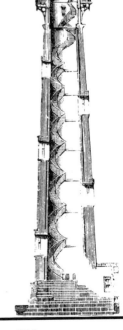

Don't let anyone go to the bathroom on your head!

There are houses in which the bathroom is right next to the bedroom. In cases like these, the principles of Feng Shui state that the head of the bed must be placed as far as possible from the bathroom door, and under no circumstances must the bed be in such a position that either its head or its foot is directly opposite the bathroom door.

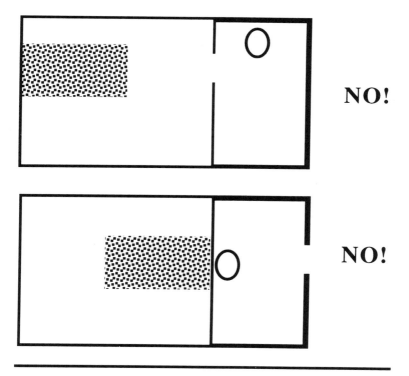

Sometimes there is a bathroom on the other side of the bedroom wall, in the same house, or - something which is extremely common - in hotels. This is bad, as the bed may well be standing with its head against the bathroom wall.

This must be rectified by moving the bed. Another case is if there is a multi-story house (or hotel), and the bedroom is located directly beneath a bathroom. Don't let anyone go to the bathroom on your head: Move the bed to another place!

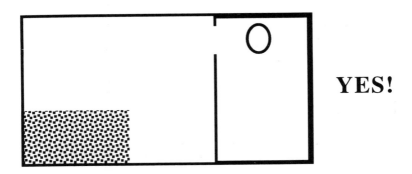

YES!

Brief advice for the basic design of the house

1. The entrance to the house, especially the front door, is the most important part of the house. Pay special attention to it!

2. The front door must fit its frame, and its height must be greater than its width.

3. The proportions of the door must be good, according to the Feng Shui rulers. The proportions of the individual components of the door - handle, lock, peepholes - must also be good.

4. The door must be in proportion to the facade of the house: Too large a door causes a shortage, while too small a door causes underhand behavior.

5. There must be light at the side of the outside door. The most desirable kind is indirect lighting on the right side of the door. The light must shine throughout the hours of darkness.

The living-room

1. The living-room should be as close as possible to the front door, but never directly opposite it. The optimal place is to the right of the entrance, but it can be on the right or the left, as long as the person who enters has to turn upon entering the living-room.

2. The main sitting area - sofa or armchairs - must not be opposite the entrance to the room, and must not be directly beneath a source of light.

3. When a person enters a room, the wall which is on his left is called "the wishing wall." Plants, mirrors, pictures or items of value should be placed along this wall.

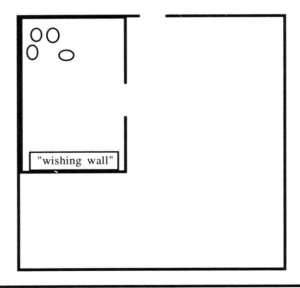

"wishing wall"

The bedroom

1. The bedroom is important for two reasons: the large amount of time we spend there every night, and the fact that most of that time we are immobile, so that the influence of the flow of energy is focused and constant.

2. If there is a bed in the bedroom (and not a mat or a mattress for sleeping), it should be raised. Use a Feng Shui ruler to check the height of the bed.

3. The head of the bed must not face the hottest side of the house. Check which the hottest side is, and avoid placing the bed in that direction.

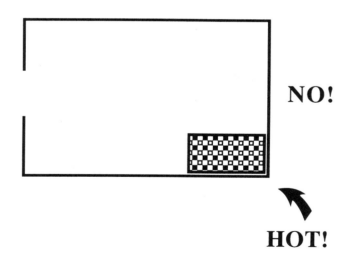

NO!

HOT!

4. The bed must not be placed directly opposite the door of the bedroom.

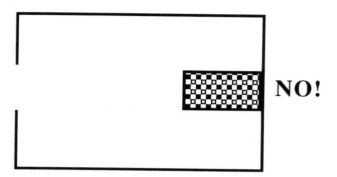

5. Check whether upon entering the bedroom, you can see the whole bed from the doorway. If you can see only part of the bed (and the rest is concealed by the door, a chest of drawers, etc.), you must rectify the situation. The whole bed must be seen!

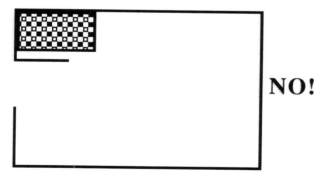

6. It is not a good idea to place the bed under a window.

7. Do not place the bed beneath a source of direct light. (You can move the light or the bed, or use a curtain or a lampshade.)

8. Do not hang a mirror opposite the entrance to the bedroom. (In fact, exposed mirrors are not recommended in the bedroom.)

9. The bedroom door must never face the kitchen directly.

10. When there are two bedrooms next to each other, they must under no circumstances be arranged in the identical way.

NO!

The kitchen

1. The preferred location of the kitchen is in the south-east corner of the house, if this is possible.

2. The kitchen is generally located at the front of the house, on the right or the left. However,in a case like this, make sure that the fireplace or the stove (the heat source) is in the south-east corner of the kitchen.

North

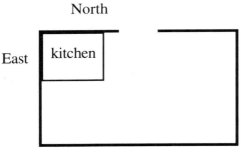

East

3. The stove (or other heat source) must not be placed opposite the kitchen entrance.

4. The distance between the kitchen and the bathroom must be as great as possible.

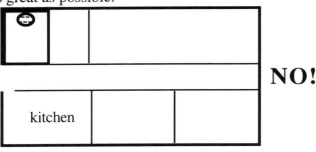

NO!

5. The kitchen must not be triangular. It must have four walls, that is, it must be square or rectangular.

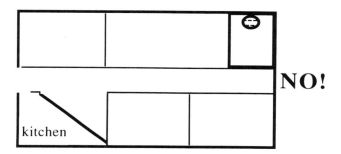

6. It is recommended that you separate the fireplace or stove (fire) and the sink (water).

The bathroom

1. This must never be in the middle of the house without external walls.

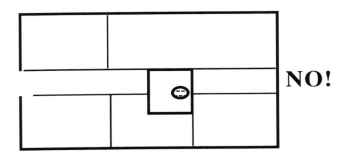

NO!

2. The further the bathroom is from the front door (and the kitchen), the better.

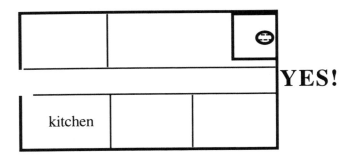

YES!

The meditation center

A meditation center, or "temple," is a place in the house where objects that are worshipped (an altar, a cross, a holy ark, etc.) or that bring back memories (photographs, trophies, souvenirs) are placed. Generally, this center is not a separate room, but is located in one of the other rooms. In the West, for example, there is a tendency to place objects of meditation on the mantelpiece.

1. The meditation center should be in the center of the house, if possible.

2. The meditation center must not be in the kitchen or bathroom.

3. The meditation center should preferably be in the corner of a room. The exact corner is selected according to the characteristics of the head of the family.

4. In the meditation center, care should be taken with the height of the table or of the shelf from the floor. (Use Feng Shui rulers.)

5. In the meditation center, there must always be an even number of objects.

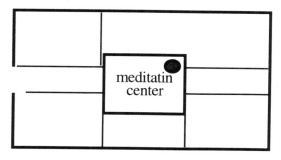

Arranging an office

1. The best location of an office is in the corner of a building, on a diagonal line from the entrance to the building.

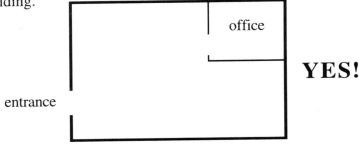

2. An office which is close to the entrance to the building, especially when only one of the walls of the office is external, is not conducive to good energy.

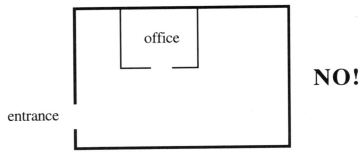

3. An office which is located at the end of a long corridor is bad for business.

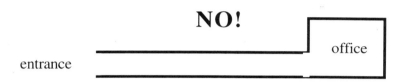

4. The best shape of an office is square. The optimum is when the height and width of all the walls are identical.

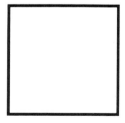

5. There must not be acute angles in an office. Even the corners of a square room should be "softened" with a sideboard, a plant, etc.

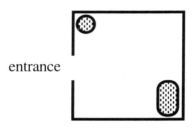

entrance

6. The center of an office is the "manager's" desk. Direct light must not shine on it.

7. An office in which there are external windows is preferable to a windowless office.

8. It is extremely undesirable for the desk to overlook a view containing acute angles (sharp roofs, towers, etc.). If this is what the view happens to be, a semi-transparent curtain should be hung.

9. No table should be placed in an office in such a way that the people who use it sit with their backs to the door.

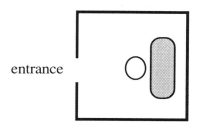

10. You should not sit in an office with your back to the window.

11. The ideal place for the desk is diagonally opposite the door to the office, so that the occupant sits facing the door.

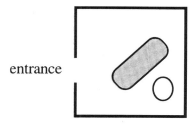

12. Shelves, filing cabinets and so on should be placed behind the occupant's chair, to his right or left, but never opposite him.

The location and design of business premises

1. The principles pertaining to a home - the location of the bathroom, for example - are valid for the location and design of business premises, too.

2. There should be other business premises in the vicinity of your business premises.

3. The business premises must never be located in a low part of the region (in a hollow), especially if there are other business premises located higher than it is.

4. The first floor of business premises - the entrance floor - must be above street level, and the difference in height must be determined and measured using Feng Shui rulers.

5. There should be a square area on the facade of the business premises, and it is even more important for there to be a small garden.

6. The door of the business premises, and the entrance to the business in general, can be much wider and higher than in a private home (in proportion to the size of the

building). The colors of the entrance are also very significant. The entrance door is the most important thing in business premises, according to Feng Shui.

7. An internal door, especially one that is opposite the entrance, must never be bigger than the entrance door.

8. The side of the tiger, according to the principles of Feng Shui, is the most suitable side for the quieter activities of the business (store-rooms, inner offices, etc.).

9. The stairs or the elevators must never be directly opposite the entrance door, but rather to the side (left or right). If the stairs or elevators are placed opposite the entrance in a building, some kind of divider should be used - a plant, for example - which will oblige the people who enter to veer off the straight path and go around the divider on their way to the stairs.

10. A clean and well-maintained facade of business premises encourages good luck.

Helping the chi flow

There are different ways to help promote the positive flow of chi.

1. Water (such as a pool, an aquarium, a vase of flowers, a fountain, or even a picture of a scene with water in it) placed on the east or south-east side.

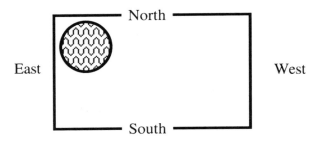

2. Sea salt, in a dish or sprinkled on the floor. This Feng Shui principle forms the basis of the belief that a pinch of salt should be put in a new house. The recommended place for the salt is on the north-east side (as well as next to the entrance of the house).

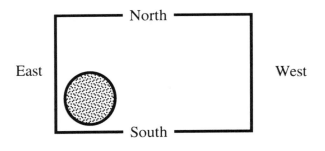

3. Metal (such as gold or iron statues, cast metal, and so on) placed on the south-west side of the house or building.

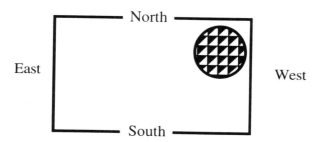

4. Plants in the form of flowerpots or small flower-beds. Plants should be placed mainly in the corners of the building, but an "avenue" consisting of two rows of plants, running from east to west, can be created.

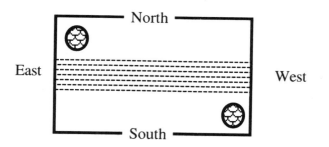

5. Use of color. The principle is simple:

On the south side, use red.

On the east side, use green.

On the north side, use black.

On the west side, use white.

A more detailed explanation is available in the charts in the book - each direction has its own particular color.

6. Mirrors and shiny surfaces (which serve as mirrors) are extremely important. Take care when setting them up.

7. Lamps and light sources are used mainly for balancing yin/yang. The principle must be twofold:

Direct light is not recommended.

Banish darkness, dim the glare.

8. Mobiles, crystals hanging on strings, or shiny metal ornaments can be hung in **open places** in the house.They augment the movement of energy (but care must be taken with other items so as to channel the energy properly).

9. There is a school of thought in Feng Shui which claims that a candle or a small fireplace must burn in the north-east corner of the building. It is totally forbidden, however, to have the candle burn in the south of the building.

10. Wind chimes, mobiles that make sounds, wind whistles and so on, are all effective in increasing chi energy. The placement of these "noisemakers" is determined by the Feng Shui Master so that they will be in harmony with the other background noises. There are no hard and fast rules about this.

11. Curtains and screens can always be used to block negative chi energy.

The Chinese Calendar

SYMBOL	DOMINANT COLOR	KI NUMBER	ASTROLOGICAL SIGN
Fire	Purple	9	Ox
Mountain	White	8	Tiger
Lake	Red	7	Rabbit
Heaven	Gray	6	Dragon
Center	Yellow	5	Snake
Wind	Blue	4	Horse
Thunder	Green	3	Ram
Earth	Black	2	Monkey
Water	Cream	1	Cock
Fire	Purple	9	Dog
Mountain	White	8	Pig
Lake	Red	7	Rat
Heaven	Gray	6	Ox
Center	Yellow	5	Tiger
Wind	Blue	4	Rabbit
Thunder	Green	3	Dragon
Earth	Black	2	Snake
Water	Cream	1	Horse
Fire	Purple	9	Ram
Mountain	White	8	Monkey
Lake	Red	7	Cock
Heaven	Gray	6	Dog
Center	Yellow	5	Pig
Wind	Blue	4	Rat
Thunder	Green	3	Ox
Earth	Black	2	Tiger
Water	Cream	1	Rabbit
Fire	Purple	9	Dragon
Mountain	White	8	Snake
Lake	Red	7	Horse
Heaven	Gray	6	Ram
Center	Yellow	5	Monkey
Wind	Blue	4	Cock
Thunder	Green	3	Dog

DOMINANT ELEMENT	BEGINNING OF YEAR (WESTERN CALENDAR)	CHINESE YEAR
Metal	2.04	1901
Water	2.05	1902
Water	2.05	1903
Wood	2.05	1904
Wood	2.04	1905
Fire	2.05	1906
Fire	2.05	1907
Earth	2.05	1908
Earth	2.04	1909
Metal	2.04	1910
Metal	2.05	1911
Water	2.05	1912
Water	2.04	1913
Wood	2.04	1914
Wood	2.05	1915
Fire	2.05	1916
Fire	2.04	1917
Earth	2.04	1918
Earth	2.05	1919
Metal	2.05	1920
Metal	2.04	1921
Water	2.04	1922
Water	2.05	1923
Wood	2.05	1924
Wood	2.04	1925
Fire	2.04	1926
Fire	2.05	1927
Earth	2.05	1928
Earth	2.04	1929
Metal	2.04	1930
Metal	2.05	1931
Water	2.05	1932
Water	2.04	1933
Wood	2.04	1934

SYMBOL	DOMINANT COLOR	KI NUMBER	ASTROLOGICAL SIGN
Earth	Black	2	Pig
Water	Cream	1	Rat
Fire	Purple	9	Ox
Mountain	White	8	Tiger
Lake	Red	7	Rabbit
Heaven	Gray	6	Dragon
Center	Yellow	5	Snake
Wind	Blue	4	Horse
Thunder	Green	3	Ram
Earth	Black	2	Monkey
Water	Cream	1	Cock
Fire	Purple	9	Dog
Mountain	White	8	Pig
Lake	Red	7	Rat
Heaven	Gray	6	Ox
Center	Yellow	5	Tiger
Wind	Blue	4	Rabbit
Thunder	Green	3	Dragon
Earth	Black	2	Snake
Water	Cream	1	Horse
Fire	Purple	9	Ram
Mountain	White	8	Monkey
Lake	Red	7	Cock
Heaven	Gray	6	Dog
Center	Yellow	5	Pig
Wind	Blue	4	Rat
Thunder	Green	3	Ox
Earth	Black	2	Tiger
Water	Cream	1	Rabbit
Fire	Purple	9	Dragon
Mountain	White	8	Snake
Lake	Red	7	Horse
Heaven	Gray	6	Ram
Center	Yellow	5	Monkey

DOMINANT ELEMENT	BEGINNING OF YEAR (WESTERN CALENDAR)	CHINESE YEAR
Wood	2.05	1935
Fire	2.05	1936
Fire	2.04	1937
Earth	2.04	1938
Earth	2.05	1939
Metal	2.05	1940
Metal	2.04	1941
Water	2.04	1942
Water	2.04	1943
Wood	2.05	1944
Wood	2.04	1945
Fire	2.04	1946
Fire	2.04	1947
Earth	2.05	1948
Earth	2.04	1949
Metal	2.04	1950
Metal	2.04	1951
Water	2.05	1952
Water	2.04	1953
Wood	2.04	1954
Wood	2.04	1955
Fire	2.05	1956
Fire	2.04	1957
Earth	2.04	1958
Earth	2.04	1959
Metal	2.05	1960
Metal	2.04	1961
Water	2.04	1962
Water	2.04	1963
Wood	2.05	1964
Wood	2.04	1965
Fire	2.04	1966
Fire	2.04	1967
Earth	2.05	1968

SYMBOL	DOMINANT COLOR	KI NUMBER	ASTROLOGICAL SIGN
Wind	Blue	4	Cock
Thunder	Green	3	Dog
Earth	Black	2	Pig
Water	Cream	1	Rat
Fire	Purple	9	Ox
Mountain	White	8	Tiger
Lake	Red	7	Rabbit
Heaven	Gray	6	Dragon
Center	Yellow	5	Snake
Wind	Blue	4	Horse
Thunder	Green	3	Ram
Earth	Black	2	Monkey
Water	Cream	1	Cock
Fire	Purple	9	Dog
Mountain	White	8	Pig
Lake	Red	7	Rat
Heaven	Gray	6	Ox
Center	Yellow	5	Tiger
Wind	Blue	4	Rabbit
Thunder	Green	3	Dragon
Earth	Black	2	Snake
Water	Cream	1	Horse
Fire	Purple	9	Ram
Mountain	White	8	Monkey
Lake	Red	7	Cock
Heaven	Gray	6	Dog
Center	Yellow	5	Pig
Wind	Blue	4	Rat
Thunder	Green	3	Ox
Earth	Black	2	Tiger
Water	Cream	1	Rabbit
Fire	Purple	9	Dragon
Mountain	White	8	Snake
Lake	Red	7	Horse

DOMINANT ELEMENT	BEGINNING OF YEAR (WESTERN CALENDAR)	CHINESE YEAR
Earth	2.04	1969
Metal	2.04	1970
Metal	2.04	1971
Water	2.05	1972
Water	2.04	1973
Wood	2.04	1974
Wood	2.04	1975
Fire	2.04	1976
Fire	2.04	1977
Earth	2.04	1978
Earth	2.04	1979
Metal	2.04	1980
Metal	2.04	1981
Water	2.04	1982
Water	2.04	1983
Wood	2.04	1984
Wood	2.04	1985
Fire	2.04	1986
Fire	2.04	1987
Earth	2.04	1988
Earth	2.04	1989
Metal	2.04	1990
Metal	2.04	1991
Water	2.04	1992
Water	2.04	1993
Wood	2.04	1994
Wood	2.04	1995
Fire	2.04	1996
Fire	2.04	1997
Earth	2.04	1998
Earth	2.04	1999
Metal	2.04	2000
Metal	2.04	2001
Water	2.04	2002

SYMBOL	DOMINANT COLOR	KI NUMBER	ASTROLOGICAL SIGN
Heaven	Gray	6	Ram
Center	Yellow	5	Monkey
Wind	Blue	4	Cock
Thunder	Green	3	Dog
Earth	Black	2	Pig
Water	Cream	1	Rat
Fire	Purple	9	Ox
Mountain	White	8	Tiger
Lake	Red	7	Rabbit
Heaven	Gray	6	Dragon
Center	Yellow	5	Snake
Wind	Blue	4	Horse
Thunder	Green	3	Ram
Earth	Black	2	Monkey
Water	Cream	1	Cock
Fire	Purple	9	Dog
Mountain	White	8	Pig
Lake	Red	7	Rat
Heaven	Gray	6	Ox
Center	Yellow	5	Tiger
Wind	Blue	4	Rabbit
Thunder	Green	3	Dragon
Earth	Black	2	Snake
Water	Cream	1	Horse
Fire	Purple	9	Ram
Mountain	White	8	Monkey

DOMINANT ELEMENT	BEGINNING OF YEAR (WESTERN CALENDAR)	CHINESE YEAR
Water	2.04	2003
Wood	2.04	2004
Wood	2.04	2005
Fire	2.04	2006
Fire	2.04	2007
Earth	2.04	2008
Earth	2.03	2009
Metal	2.04	2010
Metal	2.04	2011
Water	2.04	2012
Water	2.03	2013
Wood	2.04	2014
Wood	2.04	2015
Fire	2.04	2016
Fire	2.03	2017
Earth	2.04	2018
Earth	2.04	2019
Metal	2.04	2020
Metal	2.04	2021
Water	2.04	2022
Water	2.04	2023
Wood	2.04	2024
Wood	2.04	2025
Fire	2.04	2026
Fire	2.04	2027
Earth	2.04	2028

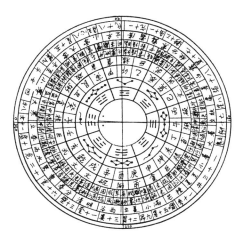